D0408164

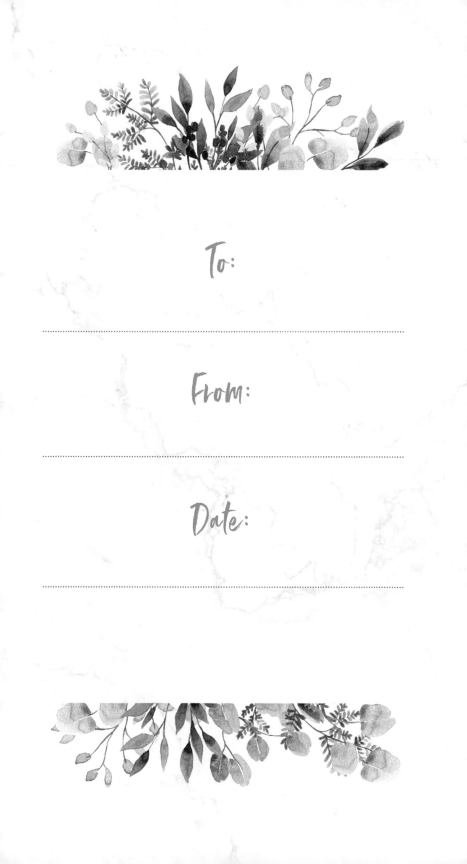

To:

....

From:

....

Date:

....

ZONDERVAN

The Weekly Gratitude Project

Copyright © 2020 by Zondervan

Requests for information should be addressed to:
Zondervan, *3900 Sparks Dr. SE, Grand Rapids, Michigan 49546*

Library of Congress Cataloging-in-Publication Data
ISBN 978-0-310-45524-0

Art direction: Tiffany Forrester
Interior design: Emily Ghattas

Printed in China

20 21 22 23 24 GRI 10 9 8 7 6 5 4 3 2 1

THE
WEEKLY GRATITUDE PROJECT

A CHALLENGE TO JOURNAL,
REFLECT, AND GROW A
GRATEFUL HEART

Contents

Promises

Gifts

Applications

How to Use This Journal

Enter his gates with thanksgiving, and his courts
with praise! Give thanks to him; bless his name!

PSALM 100:4

G ratitude, expressing it and surrounding yourself with
it, is truly life changing. God's Word and His promises
are full of His many blessings, giving us countless
reasons to voice our gratitude and thankfulness. But gratitude
can feel tough to find in a world full of busyness, neglect, and
doubt.

This book is intended to help you grow your gratitude, to
help thankfulness flourish in your life, and to expand your
heart. Each week you'll find thoughts, questions, and Scripture
verses for you to reflect on. You are encouraged to plant your
roots deep into the wonder of God's blessings, the steadfastness
of His love, and the truth of His faithfulness.

Record your thoughts, your prayers, and your gratitude
here. Take note of all the things you have to be grateful for and
all the ways you see God blessing your life. Watch how you will
steadily grow a more grateful heart and a faith that strengthens
and deepens and inspires others.

Purposeful

The Purpose of Gratitude

"Always give thanks for everything," Paul wrote in Ephesians 5:20 (TLB).

Okay, Paul, we think. *But you don't know about . . .*

No doubt you face difficult circumstances. Paul did too—we're talking stonings, shipwrecks, and starvation. He faced hard times, and because of them, he knew we'd need a reminder: always give thanks.

It takes work and intention to be grateful—to see what you have and not what you're missing, to focus on your gifts and not on your losses. It requires setting your mind on the right things and putting forth effort day by day, again and again.

It's challenging, friend. But it's so worth it.

How do we know? Paul told us, after grasping for gratitude firsthand. Even behind prison walls, Paul found gratitude a key ingredient to a hopeful perspective and a happy life. Not because it took away his chains but because it changed the way he saw them: "I am an ambassador in chains, that I may declare [the gospel] boldly" (Ephesians 6:20).

Gratitude can do the same for you. You may be stuck in difficult circumstances. The rough road you're walking may stretch for unknown miles. But gratitude can renew your mind (Romans 12:2) and transform the way you see your circumstances.

Said another way, gratitude is a new window you can use to see the world.

You may peer out and see the same old life, same old circumstances, and same old struggles. But among them, now you also see something good. Something hopeful. Something praiseworthy. Something to be thankful for.

Gratitude Transforms

*Fix your attention on God. You'll be
changed from the inside out.*

ROMANS 12:2 MSG

If only I had . . . if only I could . . .

So often we fix our attention on the "if onlys," and we're left feeling dissatisfied. But there is One who satisfies fully and forever. Fix your attention on God, and let your gratitude for Him begin to change you from the inside out.

 What are you fixated on right now? Maybe it's something that you want, or something that you lost. Write what's on your heart.

Take a deep breath and refocus your attention on God. Write about who He is, what He's done for you, what you love about Him, and why you're grateful.

*"My wayward children," says the LORD, "come back
to me, and I will heal your wayward hearts."*

JEREMIAH 3:22 NLT

Sometimes it feels like our anxious minds are the control center of our bodies. When our hearts are stuck on what brings us down, they *keep* us down—emotionally and spiritually. Gratitude is a way back up. A step toward God. A path to healing our hearts.

Can you think of ways your heart needs to heal? Are you battling discouragement, disappointment, or discontent?

Name three things you're grateful for today. Then, set a timer for two minutes and focus **only** on those things. How did this practice make you feel?

....

....

....

....

....

How might practicing an exercise like this regularly help your heart to heal?

....

....

....

Gratitude Lifts Your Spirit

*My soul . . . is bowed down within me. But this
I call to mind, and therefore I have hope: The
steadfast love of the LORD never ceases.*

LAMENTATIONS 3:20–22

When your soul feels "bowed down," like a tree that bends during a storm, how do you cope? To comfort himself, Jeremiah remembered "the steadfast love of the LORD." When you need a lift, you can do the same. Focus on God's love—a gift that is yours *no matter what.*

 Read Romans 8:31–39. Create a list of all the things that can never separate you from God's love. How does this list lift your spirit?

What other gifts from God can you be thankful for no matter what?

....

....

....

....

....

....

....

....

....

....

....

....

Disappointment Can Deflate You

*At first I didn't think of it as a gift, and begged God
to remove it. Three times I did that, and then he told
me, "My grace is enough; it's all you need. . . ." Once I
heard that, I was glad to let it happen. I quit focusing
on the handicap and began appreciating the gift.*

2 CORINTHIANS 12:9 MSG

Disappointment comes when expectations aren't met. You hope, dream, pray . . . and it doesn't happen. *Why didn't God come through?* It's okay to feel the hurt. It's okay, like Paul, to beg. But don't beg forever. Remember, you still have gifts and reasons to give thanks, and God uses your weaknesses to shine His light on you and on others.

 What struggles are you begging God to remove? How long have you been asking?

Do you think it's time to ask again, or is it time to change your focus?

 Name a gift from God that's yours **right now**. Say a prayer of thanks.

Discouragement Can Drain You

How long must I worry and feel sad in my heart all day? . . . My heart is happy because you saved me.

PSALM 13:2, 5 NCV

This psalm seems contradictory at first. Was David happy or sad? In the span of a few verses, he says both. David shows us that we can face hard seasons, ruthless enemies, and devastating losses just like him, yet still find reasons to be happy in our hearts.

When you focus only on the circumstances causing you to feel sad or to worry, why is this draining?

Despite everything you're going through, list at least ten reasons you have to be happy right now.

Losses Can Devastate You

*Job arose and tore his robe and shaved his head
and fell on the ground and worshiped.*

JOB 1:20

In verse 19, Job learned that "a great wind came . . . and struck the four corners of the house" where his children were gathered. They died—all of them, all at once. Job survived the devastating loss by finding, amid the rubble, a reason still to praise.

> What loss has been particularly devastating to you? "Cast your burden on the LORD" by writing about it honestly (Psalm 55:22).

....

....

....

....

Now write about a reason you have to praise Him. Can you think of a few more?

Gratitude Uproots Bitterness

*Today also my complaint is bitter; my hand
is heavy on account of my groaning.*

JOB 23:2

When Job's life was filled with plenty, he worshipped. But as he lost his family, his home, and his health, Job began to grow bitter. In hard seasons, bitterness can come, but *it can also go away.* (Read Job's story to the end!) Drop your cares at God's feet, not only because He cares for you (1 Peter 5:7) but because you need a place to set them down before bitterness takes root.

The Hebrews writer said, "Keep a sharp eye out for weeds of bitter discontent" (12:15 MSG). How has bitterness (either your own or someone else's) caused trouble in your life?

....

....

....

Share your cares and complaints freely with God, like Job did. How does it feel to let some things go?

Gratitude Highlights Your Gifts

For where jealousy and selfish ambition exist, there is disorder [unrest, rebellion] and every evil thing and morally degrading practice. But the wisdom from above is . . . full of compassion and good fruits.

JAMES 3:16–17 AMP

Jealousy clouds your vision. It causes you to see what someone else has or can do, forgetting all *you* have and all *you* can do. "Good fruits" come when you view others with a gracious spirit, and when you see and embrace your own gifts with gratitude.

What spiritual gift(s) has God given you? See Romans 12:6–8 for some examples.

How can you use your gift(s) to bring good fruits to God's kingdom?

....

....

....

....

....

Make a list of ways you can share good fruits with those around you. Highlight a new idea you want to try this week.

....

....

....

....

....

Gratitude Teaches Presence

Why, you do not even know what will happen tomorrow. What is your life? You are a mist that appears for a little while and then vanishes.

JAMES 4:14 NIV

When we live in the past, we drift toward regretting or romanticizing it. Live for tomorrow and the threat is anxiety—we cross our fingers for what we want or wring our hands over what we fear (Matthew 6:34). Instead, we should anchor our hearts in the present by seeing and giving thanks for our blessings.

 If the past brings you feelings of regret, consider James 5:16: "Confess your sins to one another . . . that you may be healed." What can you seek healing for today through confessing your sins?

In Matthew 6, Jesus said we need not worry because the Father takes care of us. What has God done to demonstrate His care for you?

....

....

....

....

....

Say or write a prayer of thanksgiving for your gifts.

....

....

....

....

....

....

You Will Learn Contentment

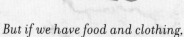

But if we have food and clothing,
with these we will be content.

1 TIMOTHY 6:8

Y ou may not have _____, but as you pray for it and wait, ask: Do I have food? Do I have clothing? Do I have four walls and a bed? Do I have freedom? Do I have forgiveness? Do I have friendships I cherish and the blessing of faith in my life?
    With what we have, may we be content.

 Those in poverty lack basic human needs: clean water, nutritious food, health care, education, clothing, and shelter (to name a few). Make a list of the basic human needs God has graciously given you.

Does your church or community offer opportunities to serve those who don't have what you do? Make a list of ways you would like to volunteer or make a donation this week.

You Will Find Joy

You have given me greater joy than those who have abundant harvests of grain and new wine.

PSALM 4:7 NLT

In verse 6 of this psalm, David wrote about people who were asking the Lord for good things. But in verse 7, it's as if he said, "Lord, You are the Good Thing!" Throughout the Bible, God shows us that joy is found less in *what* you have and more so in *whom* you have.

 Take a second to think about God. Which part of Him makes you happy or gives you joy?

Hebrews 13:8 says, "Jesus Christ is the same yesterday and today and forever." How does it make you feel to realize the joy found in Him is available to you **forever** and **whenever**?

....

....

....

....

....

In what way does this help you understand how you can "always give thanks" (Ephesians 5:20 TLB)?

....

....

....

....

....

You Will Feel Peace

*"I have told you these things so you may have peace
in Me. In the world you will have much trouble.
But take hope! I have power over the world!"*

JOHN 16:33 NLV

Like joy, your peace isn't anchored in circumstances, in being given what you want, or in life going smoothly. "In the world you will have much trouble," Jesus said. But whatever you face or whatever is lost, your peace in Jesus is stable. You can be grateful every day for that.

It doesn't make sense to feel peace when life is full of trouble. But Philippians 4:7 calls this "the peace of God, which surpasses all understanding." When have you felt God's peace in a hard season?

Read Galatians 5:22–23. Besides peace and joy, what other part of the fruit of the Spirit is yours in Christ?

....

....

....

....

....

....

....

....

....

....

....

....

Motivations

The Reasons for Gratitude

A lways give thanks for everything" (Ephesians 5:20 TLB). *Okay, Paul, but why?*

If you're a millennial, you're considered part of the "Why?" generation. Rather than easily accept authority, rules, or passed-down standards, this group asks for reasons. *Don't tell me what unless you can tell me why.*

But Paul's *why* isn't just for millennials. It's for all of us who, even though we believe, struggle to remember why we can be grateful no matter what, in every season, for everything. In another letter, we find Paul's answer:

"Give thanks whatever happens. This is what God wants for you in Christ Jesus" (1 Thessalonians 5:18 NCV).

This is what God *wants for you* in Jesus. But this is also what God *gives to you* in Jesus. Jesus is the reason we can always give thanks.

We give thanks for what He's done—especially the fact that He gave His own life so we could have eternal life in Him (John 17:2).

We give thanks for what He's promised—especially the Spirit He said would come, who has come, and who guarantees our inheritance "until we acquire possession of it" in glory (Ephesians 1:14).

And we give thanks for what He's given—especially "the forgiveness of our trespasses, according to the riches of his grace" (Ephesians 1:7).

We may not have everything we want, but friend, we have so much more than we deserve, especially in Jesus. Even before we knew Him, loved Him, or chose Him back, He chose us (Romans 5:8).

If there's nothing else on your list today, give thanks for Jesus. He is reason enough.

He Died for You

*God shows his love for us in that while we
were still sinners, Christ died for us.*

ROMANS 5:8

N o one takes it from me, but I lay it down of my own
accord" (John 10:18). Jesus said this about His *life*. He
went willingly to a Roman cross. No one forced Him to do this,
and now that it's done, no one can take away the gift of life you
receive through Him.

Describe a circumstance when you made a great
sacrifice of your time, energy, money, and/
or talents for another. What did it cost you?

What does Jesus' willingness to sacrifice **all** for you tell you about your worth?

....

....

....

....

What does His sacrifice tell you about your Savior?

....

....

....

....

....

He Made You

*For we are God's masterpiece. He has created
us anew in Christ Jesus, so we can do the
good things he planned for us long ago.*

EPHESIANS 2:10 NLT

A masterpiece isn't slapped together. Michelangelo worked more than two years to sculpt the *David*. He spent four years painting the Sistine Chapel. Ephesians 2:10 says, God "planned . . . long ago" how and when and for what He would custom craft you.

No wonder His Son gave everything to buy you back.

 A masterpiece requires time **and** a master craftsman. Do a quick search of amazing facts about creation—write down what you learn and give praise to the Designer.

How does it change how you feel about yourself knowing that you are one of God's masterpieces? That you are wonderfully made?

He Chose You

*God has chosen you and made you
his holy people. He loves you.*

COLOSSIANS 3:12 NCV

In the beginning, you were flawless . . . but "all have sinned
and fall short of the glory of God" (Romans 3:23). Even after
the cracks and stains and wear of time began to show, God
chose you. He sacrificed His only Son to restore you—in Him,
you are flawless once again.

To be chosen, whether it's for a team or for a
job, we typically have to earn it. Describe how
it feels to be chosen simply for being you.

How has walking with Jesus already helped to restore cracked, stained, or worn-out aspects of your life?

....

....

....

....

....

....

....

....

....

....

....

....

He Sought You

"The Son of Man came to seek and to save the lost."

LUKE 19:10

He made you. He liked you. He wanted you back after sin had its way with you, so He sought you. Friend, your faith in Him is no accident. It is because He's carefully pursued you. He "came to seek and to save the lost."

Write about how you came to have faith in Jesus. In your words, where do you see Him pursuing you?

....

....

....

....

....

....

How does it feel to be relentlessly
loved and sacrificially pursued?

He Leads You

*The LORD is my shepherd; I shall not want. He
makes me lie down in green pastures. He leads me
beside still waters. He restores my soul. He leads
me in paths of righteousness for his name's sake.*

PSALM 23:1–3

Jesus is more than your Savior; He's your Shepherd, which means He'll never leave your side. He paid the price to bring you into His care, and now He's watching over you and carefully leading you. You aren't left to navigate life's struggles or hard choices on your own.

What pleasant opportunities ("green pastures")
has the Lord led you to already?

....

....

....

....

In what struggle or choice do you crave His leading now?

....

....

....

....

Consider using these words in a prayer today: "When I am afraid, you, LORD, know the way" (Psalm 142:3 NCV). What other verses remind you of His leadership?

....

....

....

He Comforts You

*Even though I walk through the valley of the shadow
of death, I will fear no evil, for you are with me;
your rod and your staff, they comfort me.*

PSALM 23:4

When the way looks dark, seems treacherous, or feels too long, your Shepherd hasn't left you. He's right where He always was—still leading you, still *with* you. You can take comfort in His never-leaving presence (Hebrews 13:5).

 The shepherd's rod protects the sheep from predators. How does it comfort you to know you're being protected from enemies and evil forces (Ephesians 6:12)?

The shepherd's staff prevents the sheep from wandering. How does it comfort you to know you're being watched over and, when you need it, redirected?

He Heals You

You prepare a table before me in the presence of my enemies; you anoint my head with oil; my cup overflows.

PSALM 23:5

Another way God comforts you is by carefully watching for injuries—whether caused by stumbling, enemies, or, sometimes, other sheep. He finds you and treats you with His healing oil (James 5:14). He feeds you at a nourishing table. Your Shepherd tends your wounds.

 In what ways has walking with Jesus been healing for you?

What wound (whether physical, emotional, or spiritual) do you desire His healing for today? Talk to the Lord about it and take comfort from the words of Psalm 147:3: "He heals the brokenhearted and binds up their wounds."

He Frees You

*"So if the Son makes you free, then
you are unquestionably free."*

JOHN 8:36 AMP

A while after choosing Christ as your Shepherd, life may begin to feel like the walls are closing in—*rules, rules, rules.* You just want to be free. Friend, you are! From everything that matters, from all that can truly harm you, from death, sin, fear, and shame—you are unquestionably free!

 How is it a gift to be "set free from sin" (Romans 6:7)?

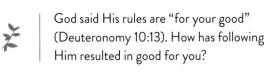

God said His rules are "for your good"
(Deuteronomy 10:13). How has following
Him resulted in good for you?

....

....

....

....

....

....

....

....

....

....

....

....

....

He Adores You

*And God raised us up with Christ and seated us
with him in the heavenly realms in Christ Jesus,
in order that in the coming ages he might show
the incomparable riches of his grace, expressed
in his kindness to us in Christ Jesus.*

EPHESIANS 2:6–7 NIV

Paul wrote, "We are . . . fellow heirs with Christ, provided we suffer with him . . . that we may also be glorified with him" (Romans 8:16–17). *Glorified* is another word for *adored*. It seems unthinkable that we're elevated to such a high place with our Shepherd.

Only a God overflowing in kindness would make such an offer.

How does it feel to realize that the same One who made you and knows you—inside and out—made a plan to glorify you in Jesus?

Even if others mistreat you, how does remembering "the great riches of [God's] loving-favor" help you find reasons to give thanks (Ephesians 2:7 NLV)?

....

....

....

....

List the reasons you're grateful because of what He's done.

....

....

....

....

....

....

Promises

What He's Promised

I will give thanks to you, LORD, with all my heart; I will tell of all your wonderful deeds" (Psalm 9:1). Maybe you've read about some of the wonderful deeds God has promised. Maybe—hopefully—you've even experienced some of those deeds for yourself.

But maybe, too, you've experienced times when you thought, *Where are You, God? Where are Your wonderful deeds now?* In seasons like these, doubt and discouragement quickly flood our hearts. We're tempted to think God's wonderful deeds are behind us. Or that they're intended for someone else.

Do not forget, friend, that God's promises do not change, even as you do. That's because they rest in His character, and who God is—loving, compassionate, merciful—does not depend on your current level of faithfulness or self-perceived worth or the season of life you are in. What God has promised, He continues to perform—now and into eternity.

Promises like, "I will send a Helper for you." Promises like, "I will return and take you home." Promises like, "You can do all things in My power." Promises like, "You may rest in My peace."

This is a short list; the Bible contains more than 3,000 of God's promises in total. Each one gives you a reason to approach the day, 365 times a year, with gratitude from the heart.

And remember, all of these wonderful deeds are guaranteed by the ultimate promise: our God is good, and His love endures forever (1 Chronicles 16:34). He has compassion for all He has made (Psalm 145:9). So in those seasons when you're not sure whether you can count on these promises, remind yourself they are not dependent on you. His character remains the same yesterday, today, and forever (Hebrews 13:8).

Your job? Tell of what He has done! Share your wonder-filled story. Bow to your loving God in worship. With a heart full of gratitude, give thanks.

A Helper

"And I will ask the Father, and He will give you another Helper (Comforter, Advocate, Intercessor—Counselor, Strengthener, Standby), to be with you forever."

JOHN 14:16 AMP

Our Shepherd knew He wouldn't be here in person forever. But before He left, He made some promises, including that He would send a Helper. This Helper lives not only with us but in us: "Your body is a temple of the Holy Spirit" (1 Corinthians 6:19).

Jesus may be out of sight for now, but our care is the closest thing to His mind.

 How has the Lord's Spirit helped, comforted, strengthened, or counseled you in the past?

....

....

....

....

Paul instructed God's people not to "quench the Spirit" (1 Thessalonians 5:19). What do you think this means? How can you invite the Spirit into your life more?

His Return

"I will not leave you as orphans; I will come to you."

JOHN 14:18

Jesus promised to send a Helper in His absence. But, friend, don't miss His promise to return! One day Jesus will be more than Someone you feel in your heart. He will be real and right in front of you, and "He will wipe away every tear from [your] eyes" (Revelation 21:4).

 Revelation 21:1–8 gives a picture of life after Jesus' return. Make a list of all that Scripture says will be "no more" (v. 1).

What do you look forward to
most about Jesus' return?

His Power

"Very truly I tell you, whoever believes in me will do the works I have been doing, and they will do even greater things than these, because I am going to the Father."

JOHN 14:12 NIV

When Jesus walked the earth, He began a work that He's now passed on to His followers (Matthew 28:19–20). If you believe in Him, you have the privilege and power to keep Jesus' work going and, as He said, to do "even greater things."

Ephesians 3:20 describes the "power at work within us" as being "able to do far more abundantly than all that we ask or think." How have you seen this power at work in your life already?

Write a prayer, thanking God for trusting you to carry on His Son's work and equipping you to carry it out.

His Peace

"I am leaving you with a gift—peace of mind and heart! And the peace I give isn't fragile like the peace the world gives. So don't be troubled or afraid."

JOHN 14:27 TLB

Doing Jesus' work isn't easy. It calls for sacrifice and, often, for choosing the harder road. Sometimes it's hard because of enemies or opposition—Jesus faced the same (John 15:18). So He promised to give us His sure, strong, able-to-withstand-the-pressure peace.

Write about a time when you faced a hardship, opposition, or loss, but you still felt God's peace that "surpasses all understanding" (Philippians 4:7).

Philippians 4:7 says, "The peace . . . will guard your hearts and your minds in Christ Jesus." Why might your heart and mind need a guardian?

....

....

....

....

....

Write a thank-you note to Jesus today for not leaving you vulnerable, but for making a way to protect you no matter what comes.

....

....

....

....

....

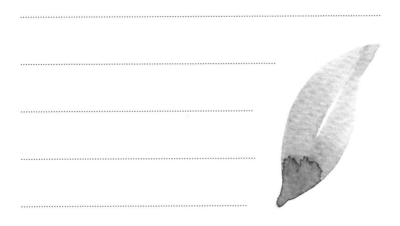

What You Need

*"When you pray, go into a room by yourself.
After you have shut the door, pray to your
Father Who is in secret. . . . Your Father knows
what you need before you ask Him."*

MATTHEW 6:6, 8 NLV

Jesus knew we'd need peace and power to stay strong in our faith. But He also knew we'd need groceries and warm clothes and the things of everyday life. He promised we could take *every* need to our Father, who gives "good things to those who ask him" (Matthew 7:11).

> What needs has the Father supplied to you spiritually? Try to list ten.

What needs has the Father supplied to you physically? Try to list ten.

....

....

....

....

....

 What needs or concerns do you want to take to the Father today? Take Jesus' advice and pray for a few minutes in secret.

....

....

....

....

....

What You Desire

*Delight yourself in the LORD, and he will
give you the desires of your heart.*

PSALM 37:4

Long before the days of Jesus, King David wrote psalms that help us understand God's will and character. Psalm 37 is one of them, reminding us that He's not a bare-minimum Father. He'll meet more than your needs—stay close to Him, and He'll bless you more than you can imagine.

> Describe a time God went over and above meeting your needs and gave you what you desired.

....

....

....

....

....

Write about one of the "desires of your heart" that you have yet to see fulfilled.

Say a prayer of thanks for God's willingness to listen to you, give to you, and meet both your wants and needs.

A Place of Rest

The promise to enter the place of rest is still good,
and we must take care that none of you miss out.

HEBREWS 4:1 CEV

Jesus' promises—what He's done—all make life here really, really good. He makes life worth living. But still, there's struggle. There's trouble. There's work, chores, and fatigue. In Jesus, we are promised a place 100 percent free of all that—a place of real, forever rest.

Think of a time when your spouse, a family member, or a friend stepped in to help you and gave you a chance to rest. Why is rest such a sweet gift?

What do you think Jesus' place of rest will be like?

A Place to Belong

"In my Father's house are many rooms. If it were not so, would I have told you that I go to prepare a place for you? And if I go and prepare a place for you, I will come again and will take you to myself, that where I am you may be also."

JOHN 14:2–3

The place of rest has "many rooms," and it's being prepared by a Shepherd who "calls his own sheep by name" (John 10:3). In other words, with Jesus, you're not nameless in a crowd or thrown forgotten in a giant room. You're seen and cared for. You have a place. You belong.

What is your favorite room in your house? Why is it your favorite?

Jesus knows your name, and He knows what you like. How does it feel to know that the One who cares for you deeply is preparing a forever home for you?

Abundance

"I came that they may have life and have it abundantly."

JOHN 10:10

Life with Jesus is a gift—not just in heaven, but *now*. Because of Him, we have a taste of abundance. We have real peace, true freedom, and pure joy. But it's only a taste (1 Corinthians 13:10). Full abundance awaits us in the promised place of rest.

How has your life become filled with blessings since you began to follow Jesus? How has He redeemed or improved your relationships, work life, habits, mental health, self-esteem, and so forth?

Write a prayer of thanks to Jesus for the abundance you have in Him now and the promise of forever blessings to come.

....

....

....

....

....

List the reasons you're grateful because of what He's promised.

....

....

....

....

....

Gifts

What He's Given

Looking ahead to what He has promised can help us. It can center us in the good to come, no matter the bleakness that sometimes darkens our hearts or fills our days. But we don't have to look ahead.

Good things are all around you *right now!*

What He's already given is more than what He's promised to give in the future. Consider, for instance, the gift of grace, which Paul said "is the gift of God, not a result of works, so that no one may boast" (Ephesians 2:8–9). This grace is *already* yours in Christ. You are *already* a new creation because of it, able to live a better life and make better choices than you've ever made before.

Consider the gift of hope. When Paul wrote to the Romans, he said we could "rejoice in hope" (12:12). This reason to rejoice is not yours to come. It's yours *now*. It's why you can open your eyes right now—in *this* day—with a smile on your face and joy in your heart.

Consider what Paul described as "the greatest" gift of all (1 Corinthians 13:13). If God's love is already—and always—for us, what other gifts could we possibly need?

When packing your bags for a vacation, you're likely to include a camera, or at least, you're sure to pack a phone. This is because you *anticipate* seeing something worth capturing, something worth turning into a memory because of its uniqueness or beauty or both.

What if we approached every day this way?

But, instead of with a camera, what if we approached each day with a focused heart? What if we adjusted our lens so we could see the gifts God has placed all around us—little and big, invisible and visible, spiritual and physical, recurring and unique to today?

We have countless reasons to be thankful—but *do start counting!* Open your eyes to all He has given and give thanks.

Grace

*In him we have redemption through his
blood, the forgiveness of sins, in accordance
with the riches of God's grace.*

EPHESIANS 1:7 NIV

Grace—it's the best gift we have and maybe the hardest gift to understand because it's so unlike anything else. It never wears out. It never quits working. It's ours, even though we don't deserve it. It's ours, even when we forget we have it. It's the ultimate reason to be grateful.

> Describe "God's rich grace." What is it? What has it done for you? What does it continue to do?

Is God's rich grace a gift you can
share with others? How?

Hope

So now faith, hope, and love abide, these three.

1 CORINTHIANS 13:13

Hope is fuel. It's what keeps us going when the days are hard. It's what keeps us believing when valleys are long. It's why we get back up, pushing on in faith, expecting better days to come. And they will. Because our hope is anchored in the One whom hard days and long valleys can't touch: "In Christ we have hope" (1 Corinthians 15:19).

 The book of Hebrews talks about all the "better" things Christ brings to life—both here and in heaven. How has Christ already made your life better?

What's something in your life that you
hope is made better in the future?

....

....

....

....

 We don't know how some things will turn out,
but we do know about others. What do you
hope for that's "sure and steadfast," promised
to come about in Jesus (Hebrews 6:19)?

....

....

....

....

....

....

love

*So now faith, hope, and love abide, these
three; but the greatest of these is love.*

1 CORINTHIANS 13:13

Hope is fuel to carry us to tomorrow; love is a gift to carry us through today. Whatever we're facing, whatever we wish we had or wish we didn't have, whatever trouble or pain comes today, love comes too. It's higher, wider, and deeper than any other thing.

And it's here to stay (Romans 8:38–39).

> Why do you think Paul said love is "the greatest" in 1 Corinthians 13:13?

What are you facing today that's troubling you? Write about it, and then on top of what you've written, around and all over it, write the words "I am loved."

A Family

*Consequently, you are no longer foreigners
and strangers, but fellow citizens with God's
people and also members of his household.*

EPHESIANS 2:19 NIV

In Christ, you have the gift of God's love, and you have the love of a family—God's family. Each body of believers offers brothers and sisters, mentors and friends to remind you of your value, hope, and purpose and to encourage you every step of faith's way.

Think about the church family to which you belong—what are its strengths? What are you thankful for?

....

....

....

....

....

If you don't attend a church regularly, what's holding you back? How might becoming a member of a family be a blessing to you?

....

....

....

....

....

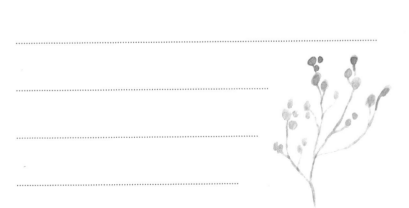

Make a list of the people within God's family who've made a significant impact on your life, faith, and well-being.

....

....

....

....

....

Help

Brothers and sisters, if someone is caught in a sin, you who live by the Spirit should restore that person gently. But watch yourselves, or you also may be tempted. Carry each other's burdens, and in this way you will fulfill the law of Christ.

GALATIANS 6:1–2 NIV

God's family is a support system: "A cord of three strands is not quickly broken" (Ecclesiastes 4:12 NIV). But God's family is *much* larger than three. It's hundreds of thousands of millions around the globe. What a gift it is to be carried by so many through life's ups and downs.

 What burdens (troubles and problems) has God's family helped carry you through in the past?

Is there something you need help with now—a decision, struggle, temptation, or painful circumstance? Whom in God's family could you reach out to?

....

....

....

....

Who in God's family might you be able to help?

....

....

....

....

....

....

Friends

*A friend is always loyal, and a brother
is born to help in time of need.*

PROVERBS 17:17 NLT

Who is your "time of need" friend? The one who's been with you through the valleys? Maybe you have more than one. Those people, those friends, are gifts. They didn't come into your life accidentally. Be thankful to God for every single one.

> Write about one of your "time of need" friends. Why are you thankful to know him or her?

....

....

....

....

Make a list of other friends you're thankful to have in your life. Beside each name, write a word or phrase that describes what you appreciate about the individual.

Food to Eat

*"Every moving thing that lives shall be food for you. And
as I gave you the green plants, I give you everything."*

GENESIS 9:3

Maybe your pantry isn't as full as you'd like. Maybe you can't afford to eat out every week, or maybe you can. Whatever you have—in times of "plenty and hunger, abundance and need"—is a gift (Philippians 4:12).

 Are you facing a season of abundance or
need right now? How has God shown Himself
faithful to provide in this season?

Write about your favorite food or drink—can you treat yourself to something today? As you do, give thanks to God, who so often goes beyond your needs to supply your desires.

Clothes to Wear

"But if God so clothes the grass of the field, which today is alive and tomorrow is thrown into the oven, will he not much more clothe you, O you of little faith?"

MATTHEW 6:30

Don't compare clothing brands. Don't worry about the age of those jeans. Is your body covered? Are you warm? Are you even able to express some personality and wear different clothes and colors from day to day and week to week? You've been given a gift!

What's your favorite piece of clothing you own? Why do you like it?

90

Write a prayer of thanks for the clothes you own, however outdated or worn out they might be.

....

....

....

....

....

Look around your home today. What other gifts has God provided?

....

....

....

....

....

....

Spiritual Gifts

To one there is given through the Spirit a message of wisdom, to another a message of knowledge by means of the same Spirit, to another faith by the same Spirit, to another gifts of healing by that one Spirit, to another miraculous powers, to another prophecy, to another distinguishing between spirits, to another speaking in different kinds of tongues, and to still another the interpretation of tongues. All these are the work of one and the same Spirit, and he distributes them to each one, just as he determines.

1 CORINTHIANS 12:8–11 NIV

I f you can't do everything on the list in today's verses, that's okay—you weren't meant to! When Christ adds you to His body, He fills you with His Spirit, and His Spirit presents you with gifts to complement the larger whole. You might have one gift or several—use them all for Christ!

 Do you know your spiritual gift(s)? If you aren't sure, reread Paul's list from 1 Corinthians 12:8–11, and write about any that resonate with you.

What spiritual gifts do you see others in your life displaying, whether in your church family or in your home?

Opportunities

Whenever we have the opportunity, we should do good to everyone—especially to those in the family of faith.

GALATIANS 6:10 NLT

Friend, Jesus died not only to save you but also to fill your life with purpose. He trusted you with gifts and grants you opportunities to use them. Look around. Pay attention. Ask God to open your eyes and help you step into the role He created only *you* to fulfill.

 What opportunities has God opened for you in the past to use your spiritual gifts?

What opportunities are available today for you to do good, especially showing goodness to someone belonging to the family of faith?

....

....

....

....

List below the reasons why you're grateful for the gifts He's given to you.

....

....

....

....

....

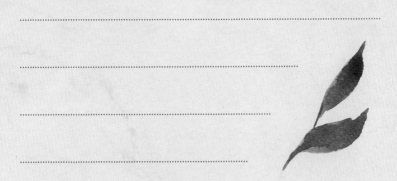

Applications

The Practice of Gratitude

Always give thanks for everything" (Ephesians 5:20 TLB). We know why. We know for what. But now we're asking, *How?* How do we give thanks when our world is falling apart? How do we give thanks when our lives are so busy? How do we give thanks when we don't *feel* thankful?

Gratitude begins with a choice: *I am going to set my mind.*

Set your mind on all the reasons you've already listed—what He's done, what He's promised, and what He's given. Keep setting your mind on those gifts day by day. Then, add to your list. Write down each gift as you recognize it. Go back and reread your list so that you will remember—on the hard days, on the easy days, on the busy days—all your many reasons to be grateful.

You have a choice. You can walk through life with your head down, wondering why you don't have *this* and questioning whether you'll ever have *that.* Or you can look up, smile, and see that life in Jesus is a gift . . .

Every. Single. Day.

Life in Jesus means hope, peace, and abundance *no matter what.* It means you are loved and taken care of and well supplied. It means you can let go of every worry and cast aside every fear.

So choose gratitude, and make gratitude the daily foundation you build upon: *Whatever else happens today, Jesus is mine, and I am thankful.* Invest in that foundation morning, noon, and night. Nurture it until it takes full bloom.

"Blessed is the man who trusts . . . [and] the woman who sticks with GOD. They're like trees replanted in Eden, putting down roots near the rivers—never a worry through the hottest of summers, never dropping a leaf, serene and calm through droughts, bearing fresh fruit every season" (Jeremiah 17:8 MSG).

May your fruit be sweet offerings of thanksgiving.

Set Your Mind

Set your minds on things that are above,
not on things that are on earth.

COLOSSIANS 3:2

The mindset of gratitude doesn't happen by accident. It's not something you'll stumble into, no matter how godly your friends are or how often you go to church. You have to *choose* to be grateful. And gratitude becomes a habit when you keep choosing it day by day.

When has gratitude come to you naturally?

When has gratitude been hard for you to feel or express?

....

....

....

....

....

What can you do to choose gratitude every day, no matter what?

....

....

....

....

....

Start a List

*For everything God created is good, and nothing is
to be rejected if it is received with thanksgiving.*

1 TIMOTHY 4:4 NIV

Y ou've already begun this practice. Now, keep it going. Find a notebook or a blank piece of paper. Start with at least three new entries each day, asking yourself, "What am I thankful for?" Think big. Think small. Write down your many reasons to give thanks.

 What are three small things you're thankful for today (e.g., coffee in the morning, a warm bed to sleep in, a coworker's act of kindness, or reading with your child)?

What are three big things you're thankful for today (e.g., God's grace, safety provided by first responders, or your relationship with your spouse or best friend)?

Grow Your List

*Devote yourselves to prayer, being
watchful and thankful.*

COLOSSIANS 4:2 NIV

Add to your list day by day. This is key. Once you've done this a while, you might start repeating yourself. That's okay! A gift that's returned every morning—grace, sunrises, breath—is no less valuable. So write the rare things; write the recurring things. Keep giving thanks.

 What are some rare gifts you've received in the last year (e.g., a new opportunity, a relationship, or a season of spiritual growth)?

What are some recurring gifts you receive each day or each week (e.g., food, a paycheck, health insurance, or the ability to walk)?

Read and Remember

I have not stopped giving thanks for you,
remembering you in my prayers.

EPHESIANS 1:16 NIV

Some days are harder than others. When discouragement clouds our vision, we can forget our many reasons to give thanks. This is when your list comes in handy—and why it's important to have a list! On the days you need help, read and be reminded of your gifts.

 Spend a few minutes rereading the gifts you've written down in this journal. Which gifts stand out to you? How do you feel after reading through them?

....

....

....

....

....

Make a game plan for the discouraging or disappointing days that will inevitably come. How will you set your mind on gratitude, even when you don't feel grateful?

Give Thanks Out Loud

*All the angels were standing around the throne and
around the elders and the four living creatures,
and they fell on their faces before the throne and
worshiped God, saying, "Amen! Blessing and glory
and wisdom and thanksgiving and honor and power
and might be to our God forever and ever! Amen."*

REVELATION 7:11–12

You might know something in your mind, but it becomes
tangible and sticks with you when you write it down. The
same can be said for repeating something out loud. It's another
way to solidify the truth in your heart that you have so many
reasons to give thanks.

> Spend a few minutes reading out loud the gifts
> you've written down so far. How did reading them
> aloud affect your mindset and your mood?

Did you think of more gifts during the process?
Write them down—and say them out loud too!

Give Thanks Before Others

*Whenever the living creatures give glory and honor
and thanks to him who is seated on the throne, who
lives forever and ever, the twenty-four elders fall down
before him who is seated on the throne and worship
him who lives forever and ever. They cast their crowns
before the throne, saying, "Worthy are you, our Lord
and God, to receive glory and honor and power."*

REVELATION 4:9–11

You've written down your gifts. You've said your gifts out loud. Now it's time to take what you've come to know yourself and make it real for others. Choose a friend, coworker, child, or relative. Tell him or her a reason—or several reasons—why you're grateful. Your honesty will bless you both.

 What are your thoughts about expressing your gratitude to someone else? Are you hesitant or eager? Why do you think you feel this way?

Do you have someone you can share your thoughts and feelings with? Do you know how you want to share your thankful heart? Write it down here first, like you're writing a letter. You don't need to be formal; just describe why you're grateful.

Learn Others' Needs

*Religion that is pure and undefiled before God the
Father is this: to visit orphans and widows in their
affliction, and to keep oneself unstained from the world.*

JAMES 1:27

Compassion is at the heart of God's will for you; it's also a compass, pointing you back to gratitude. When you're sad about losses, when you're stuck on disappointments, or when setting your mind on gifts doesn't help, set your mind on others' needs.

How do you typically handle a season
of discouragement or despair?

....

....

....

....

....

How might focusing on others' needs redirect
your thinking back toward gratitude?

Become a Servant

*"For I was hungry and you gave me food, I
was thirsty and you gave me drink, I was a
stranger and you welcomed me, I was naked
and you clothed me, I was sick and you visited
me, I was in prison and you came to me."*

MATTHEW 25:35–36

When you're stuck feeling ungrateful, it's helpful to shift your focus to others' needs. But it's even better to get involved and do what you can to meet those needs. You will change how you see your life and gifts. Better still, you will *be* a gift to another.

 How does serving others change the way you see your life, gifts, losses, and problems?

....

....

....

....

Who in your life can you serve this week?
(Here are some ideas: send a card, make a
phone call, plan a visit, or help with a chore.)

Go Back to the Basics

*"Remember, therefore, what you have
received and heard; hold it fast."*

REVELATION 3:3 NIV

Sometimes it's just too hard of a day, or you're just too caught up in the devastation happening around you to see the good. Don't give up. Go back to the basics. Focus on the sure things—the gifts that will never go away. You *always* have reasons to give thanks.

> What sure things can you be grateful for, no matter what?

....

....

....

....

Hebrews 13:8 says, "Jesus Christ is the same yesterday and today and forever." How does this truth bring you peace and make you grateful?

Offer a Sacrifice

*Through him then let us continually offer up
a sacrifice of praise to God, that is, the fruit
of lips that acknowledge his name. Do not
neglect to do good and to share what you have,
for such sacrifices are pleasing to God.*

HEBREWS 13:15–16

Always having a reason to give thanks doesn't mean giving thanks is always easy. Some days, choosing gratitude for sure things—because desired things are off the table—is a sacrifice. It's a pledge we make even when we don't feel it because we know, no matter how we feel, God is worthy of our praise.

> What do you think it means to offer a sacrifice of thanksgiving to God?

Have you ever made a sacrifice of thanksgiving to God? Are you in a season where it would be a sacrifice to praise and thank God now?

....

....

....

....

....

Write a prayer of thanksgiving.

....

....

....

....

....

....

Begin with Gratitude

*And whatever you do, whether in word or deed,
do it all in the name of the Lord Jesus, giving
thanks to God the Father through him.*

COLOSSIANS 3:17 NIV

Gratitude takes root and grows fruit when you set your mind on it and return to it day by day. To remember to do this, begin your days, prayers, or conversations with gratitude. Just keep gratitude at the forefront of your mind.

> What would it look like to begin your days,
> prayers, or conversations with gratitude?
> Which seems the most doable to you?

Why do you think giving thanks "in all you do" makes God happy?

End with Gratitude

*As you received Christ Jesus the Lord, so
walk in him, rooted and built up in him
and established in the faith, just as you
were taught, abounding in thanksgiving.*

COLOSSIANS 2:6–7

Plant your roots and build them up by letting gratitude become not only the way you begin but the way you end too. Don't go to bed with negativity (Ephesians 4:26). Our God is too good and His gifts are too great for us ever to run out of reasons to give thanks.

> What might it look like to close out your days, prayers, or conversations with gratitude? Which seems the most doable to you?

Why do you think it's important to remember God is always worthy of thanks?